GLOWWORMS ARE NOT WORMS!

Daisy Allyn

Gareth Stevens
PUBLISHING

Please visit our website, www.garethstevens.com. For a free color catalog of all our high-quality books, call toll free 1-800-542-2595 or fax 1-877-542-2596.

Library of Congress Cataloging-in-Publication Data

Allyn, Daisy.
Glowworms are not worms! / by Daisy Allyn.
p. cm. — (Confusing creature names)
Includes index.
ISBN 978-1-4824-0942-0 (pbk.)
ISBN 978-1-4824-0943-7 (6-pack)
ISBN 978-1-4824-0941-3 (library binding)
1. Fireflies — Juvenile literature. I. Allyn, Daisy. II. Title.
QL596.L28 A44 2015
595.76—d23

Published in 2015 by
Gareth Stevens Publishing
111 East 14th Street, Suite 349
New York, NY 10003

Designer: Michael J. Flynn
Editor: Greg Roza

Photo credits: Cover Joerg Hauke/Picture Press/Getty Images; p. 5 (common glowworm) Henrik Larsson/Shutterstock.com; p. 5 (firefly) ivkuzmin/Thinkstock.com; p. 7 http://en.wikipedia.org/wiki/File:Leuchtk%C3%A4fer_-_Firefly.JPG; p. 9 Stephen Dalton/Minden Pictures/Getty Images; p. 11 James Jordan Photography/Flickr/Getty Images; p. 13 Gail Shumway/Photographer's Choice/Getty Images; p. 15 (main image) Stuart Wilson/Photo Researchers/Getty Images; p. 15 (inset) Dr. Morley Read/Getty Images; p. 17 (fireflies) Fer Gregory/Shutterstock.com; p. 17 (glass jar) Carsten Reisinger/Shutterstock.com; p. 19 Carsten Peter/National Geographic/Getty Images; p. 21 Suzanne Tucker/Shutterstock.com.

Printed in the United States of America

CPSIA compliance information: Batch #CS15GS: For further information contact Gareth Stevens, New York, New York at 1-800-542-2595.

CONTENTS

Boldface words appear in the glossary.

Worms or Bugs?

Glowworms aren't worms—they're bugs. Many kinds of glowworms live all over the world. Most glowworms are kinds of beetles. Some glowworms are gnats, which are very tiny flies. Have you ever seen a firefly? Then you've seen one kind of glowworm!

common glowworm

firefly

Glowing Babies

Many baby insects look like worms. At this **stage** of life, they're called larvae (LAHR-vee). A single baby insect is called a larva (LAHR-vuh). The larvae of some insects can glow. This is where the name "glowworm" comes from.

7

Glowing Girls

Not all glowworms are baby bugs. Some are adult female bugs. They still look like larvae, though. And they still glow. They're called larvaform adults. Some kinds of female fireflies are larvaform adults.

9

How Do They Glow?

Glowworms have special body parts that allow them to light up. This part is different in different types of glowworms. But most glowing parts work in a similar way. The glow is caused by **chemicals** mixing inside the bug's body.

11

Why Do They Glow?

Some glowworms glow to catch food. Small critters see the light and come close to check it out. That's when the glowworm catches its **prey**. Some female glowworms light up to **attract** males. Others light up to warn predators that they're not good to eat.

13

Beetles

Most glowworms are beetles. Click beetles make a clicking sound, and some can glow, too. They're often just called glowworm beetles. The railroad worm is another common glowing beetle. Both larvae and adult female railroad worms glow.

click beetle

15

You might be surprised to hear that fireflies aren't flies at all—they're glowing beetles! Both the larvae and females glow. Females, which are often wingless, blink their lights to attract males. However, males are often tricked by streetlights!

Fantastic Fireflies!

Fireflies are found on every continent except Antarctica.

Some kinds of firefly eggs glow, too.

Most adult fireflies live long enough to lay eggs, then they die. Some adults don't even have time to eat!

Some fireflies are known to copy the glow and flash of other fireflies. They may do this to scare away other fireflies or to attract them.

17

Gnats

About a dozen kinds of gnats glow. Many live on the walls and ceilings of caves in New Zealand and Australia. The glowing larvae hang from the ceiling by sticky threads. Other bugs become trapped on the threads, and the larvae eat them for dinner.

19

Turning Off?

Some scientists think glowworms are in danger of dying out. Growing towns and cities have changed many glowworm **habitats**. Streetlights can confuse males searching for female glowworms, leading to fewer babies. Can you think of any ways to help keep glowworms safe?

GLOSSARY

attract: to draw nearer

chemical: matter that can be mixed with other matter to cause changes

habitat: the natural place where an animal or plant lives

prey: an animal that is hunted by other animals for food

stage: one part of an animal's life

FOR MORE INFORMATION

BOOKS

Spilsbury, Richard. *Zoom in on Bizarre Bugs.* Berkeley Heights, NJ: Enslow Publishers, 2013.

Stewart, Melissa. *Zoom in on Fireflies.* Berkeley Heights, NJ: Enslow Publishers, 2014.

WEBSITES

Firefly
www.environmentalgraffiti.com/featured/bioluminescent-insects-glowing-darkness/15236
Read much more about fireflies, as well as how you can help protect them.

Story: Glow-worms
www.teara.govt.nz/en/glow-worms/page-1
Learn more about the glowing larvae of the fungus gnat found in caves in New Zealand and Australia.

INDEX